TH
EQUAL-BE
TEMPERAMENTS

A HANDBOOK
FOR TUNING HARPSICHORDS AND FORTE-PIANOS,
WITH TUNING TECHNIQUES AND
TABLES OF FIFTEEN HISTORICAL TEMPERAMENTS

BY

OWEN JORGENSEN

RALEIGH:
THE SUNBURY PRESS
1981

23.75

Library of Congress Cataloging in Publication Data

Jorgensen, Owen.
    The equal-beating temperaments.

    Bibliography: p.
    Includes index.
    1. Keyboard instruments—Tuning. 2. Musical
temperament. I. Title.
MT165.J66   786.2'3   81-662
ISBN 0-915548-12-7   AACR2

PRINTED FOR THE SUNBURY BY BYNUM PRINTING COMPANY: RALEIGH.

TABLE OF CONTENTS

The need for temperament

Sounds are classified as either chaotic noise or sustained musical tones. The psychological response produced from a musical tone is defined as a pitch. The pitches emitted from musical instruments are identified by letter names such as A, B, C, etc. A musical tone consists of its loud basic pitch and also many softer higher pitches that sound together with the fundamental. The relative strengths or weaknesses of these various pitches determine the timbre of the tone. The fundamental pitch along with the higher pitches or overtones are collectively known as harmonics. Harmonics are governed by natural laws that cause them to form an acoustic series as follows: The first harmonic is the fundamental pitch. The second harmonic has a frequency twice that of the fundamental and is an octave higher in pitch. The third harmonic has a frequency three times that of the fundamental and is an octave plus a fifth higher in pitch. The fourth harmonic has a frequency four times that of the fundamental and is two octaves higher in pitch. The fifth harmonic has a frequency five times that of the fundamental and is two octaves plus a major third higher in pitch. This series can go on indefinitely.

Each tone of an interval contains its own harmonic series. Pitches that are common to both of the series determine whether the interval is in tune. If the frequencies of these pitches are identical, then the interval is in tune, and no beating or pulsating is heard. This kind of interval is known as a just interval. An example of a just interval is as follows: If the frequency of A is 220 Hertz, then A's fifth harmonic has a frequency of 1100 Hertz. If C-sharp has a frequency of 275 Hertz, then C-sharp's fourth harmonic has a frequency of 1100 Hertz. Since the fifth harmonic of A is identical to the fourth harmonic of C-sharp, there is no difference between the harmonics, there is no beating, and the interval is completely in tune as in just intonation. Thus the ratio of a just major third is 5 to 4, often written as 1.25. A at 220 Hertz times 1.25 equals 275 Hertz, which is exactly the frequency of C-sharp in the above example. Continuing further, 275 Hertz times 1.25 equals 343.75, which is the frequency of E-sharp, a just major third above C-sharp. Continuing once more, 343.75 Hertz times 1.25 equals 429.6875 Hertz, which is the frequency of G-double sharp, a just major third above E-sharp. The ratio of a just octave is 2 to 1, often written as 2. A at 220 Hertz times 2 equals 440 Hertz, which is the frequency of another A, a just octave above the lower A. Notice the difference in frequency between the A at 440 and the G-double sharp at 429.6875 Hertz.

The above example shows that three just major thirds do not add up to make a just octave. Similar examples show that four just minor thirds do not create one just octave, twelve just fourths do not equal five just octaves, and twelve just fifths do not match seven just octaves. Since it is traditional in Western music to tune octaves in just intonation, and since no series of just intervals will ever match one or more just octaves, a compromising system known as tempering is necessary to make all the intervals usable on keyboard instruments. Tempered intervals are mistuned from just intonation in a controlled manner in order to effect these compromises. Because of this intentional mistuning, tempered intervals sound unstable, and they pulsate. These pulsations or vibrations among the harmonics are known as beats.

The historical temperaments

The history of temperament is the history of the extent that the just intervals on keyboard instruments were compromised for the sake of practicality. No compromising was done until the late fifteenth century, when a few just intervals were tempered very cautiously. Later, the practice of compromising the just intervals was applied gradually more and more until the nineteenth and twentieth centuries, when all the just intervals except the octave were tempered in the modern equal temperament.

It is evident that there were never any improvements in temperament, only changes. For every utilitarian gain there was a corresponding loss of just intonation. In the early just intonations and the meantone temperaments, the octave C to C, the major third C E, and the major third E G-sharp were all tuned to just intonation. The result was that the diminished fourth G-sharp C was extremely out of tune. This interval was called a wolf because it howled or beat so rapidly that it could not be used in musical performance. When historical development later corrected G-sharp C barely enough so that it could be used as a good major third A-flat C, the major third E G-sharp had to be compromised so that it was almost as tempered as the new A-flat C. Still later, in order to improve E G-sharp, the commonly-used major third C E was compromised to a small extent. Finally, during the nineteenth century, the major thirds C E, E G-sharp, and A-flat C were all tempered equally, and all traces of the stability of just intonation were lost.

The historical tunings and temperaments are divided into five classifications. First, Pythagorean tuning was used from the beginning of keyboard instruments through the Renaissance. Second, the theoretical complete just intonation tuning had very limited use during the sixteenth and seventeenth centuries. Third, meantone temperament was used extensively from the beginning of the sixteenth century into the early eighteenth century. For basic music, meantone temperament continued into the nineteenth century. Fourth, the well-temperaments dominated most performance practice in Germany from the late seventeenth century into the early nineteenth century. Fifth, various quasi-equal temperaments were practiced throughout much of the nineteenth century. Equal temperament as we know it was not practiced until late in the nineteenth century. A sixth classification includes avant-garde or contemporary temperaments such as the five and seven temperament published in 1973 by Owen Jorgensen.

Interpreting the historical temperaments

Musicians have developed by observing the works of other masters and by applying their own instincts and good taste through practice and experience. The endeavors of musicians are channeled into artistic creativity rather than the study of mathematics, physics, and acoustics. Therefore, the information that exists on tempering methods of the past was recorded by theorists and rarely by the great composers themselves. When theorists described on paper what the musicians were doing (or what the theorists thought they ought to be doing), the methods were described in exact mathematical terms. These mathematics are recorded in the book *Tuning and Temperament* by J. Murray Barbour, Michigan State College Press, East Lansing, 1953. When tuning is done according to strict mathematical models, the methods are known as theoretically correct temperaments. These demand the ultimate precision and cross-checking of all intervals for the exact numbers of beat speeds. The modern equal temperament is an example of a theoretically correct temperament, and it requires the abilities of a professional piano technician. All the theoretically correct temperaments that are practical to tune by ear are outlined in the book *Tuning the Historical Temperaments by Ear* by Owen Jorgensen, the Northern Michigan University Press, Marquette, 1977. These theoretical temperaments are somewhat historical, but a step closer to authenticity is to interpret these temperaments according to the easy instinctive methods that musicians actually used. Applying these methods results in the equal-beating temperaments. Paralleling many of the theoretical temperaments in *Tuning the Historical Temperaments by Ear* are the equal-beating interpretations of the same temperaments. Equal-beating methods that are as close as possible to the original theoretical ideals were used. Nine of the first ten tuning and equal-beating temperament methods listed in the following pages are selected and reprinted from *Tuning the Historical Temperaments by Ear* by permission from the Northern Michigan University Press.

The difference between the theoretically correct methods and the equal-beating methods is described in the following example. If one expected to temper D between a lower B-flat and an upper F-sharp and if the theoretically correct method were to be used, then the tuner must refer to a chart of beat speeds for that particular temperament, and calculated for one particular pitch, to determine what the beat speeds for B-flat D and D F-sharp should be. The beat speeds are always different for two theoretical thirds, or for the same third at two different pitches, and the next step is to temper D until the beat speeds are correct according to the chart. This requires experience. Cross-checking of beat speeds of all the tempered intervals is then applied to determine if any errors were made. This demands a thorough knowledge of the acoustics of the particular temperament. It is obvious that musicians of past centuries rarely applied these theoretical methods, and their writings seldom mention beat speeds. Instead they tempered instinctively by adjusting D between the lower B-flat and upper F-sharp until the major thirds B-flat D and D F-sharp sounded identical in quality. In the latter case, the beat speeds of B-flat D and D F-sharp would become identical, but musicians were not concerned about what the resulting beat frequencies were supposed to be. They did not need this information; the technique of tuning a third tone so that it is equal-beating works independently of the pitch of the interval. This instinctive method of tempering is known as the equal-beating method. The musicians of past centuries, and many of the theorists as well, thought that the equal-beating method produced major thirds that were the same size, because they sounded identical in quality. The truth is that the third B-flat D was very slightly larger than the third D F-sharp in order to create the equal-beating effect. The equal-beating methods are more musical than the theoretically correct methods.

The first five equal-beating well-temperament methods listed in this book should be considered the same as the eighteenth-century charts of ornaments; that is, like the charts, they are documented performance practices. These five well temperaments can be used authentically for all composers from Buxtehude through early Beethoven. Choosing which well-temperament to use for the music is a matter of personal taste.

Like the ornamentation charts, the five well-temperaments also serve as examples that may be varied according to good taste with discretion. Applying these eighteenth-century principles to the temperaments resulted in the common model well-temperament and the final temperaments in this book. The common model temperament is called a Bendeler-Young composite because it is a hybrid between the Bendeler and Young temperaments. The primary thirds C E, F A, and G B from the composite are similar to those in Andreas Werckmeister's Correct

Temperament No. 2, published in 1691. A large number of intervals that are common to each of the five basic well-temperaments mentioned above and also to many other eighteenth- and early nineteenth-century temperaments have been incorporated into the Bendeler-Young composite. Thus, this composite is a very representative eighteenth-century type of well-temperament that is appropriate for all eighteenth-century Germanic music.

The criteria for determining the authenticity of a well-temperament are the degree of ease in setting the temperament and the faithfulness to Werckmeister's principles (see page 21). The Bendeler-Young composite fulfills these requirements superbly. The Bendeler-Young composite and the other final well-temperaments in this book contain the superior musical qualities whereby the major thirds F A and G B each beat the same speed because they are from tonic triads with equal musical values from keys with one accidental each. Also, the major thirds B-flat D and D F-sharp each beat the same speed because they are from tonic triads with equal musical values from keys with two accidentals each.

The well-temperaments on pages 30 and 31 of this book are intended for those tuners who wish to apply their own personal taste to greater degrees while still producing authentically historical results.

Tuning techniques

Tuning one's own instrument is an excellent ear training exercise that has been sadly neglected by most keyboard performers for well over a century. Tuning harpsichords or other early keyboard instruments is not difficult because the string tensions and frictions at the bearing points are significantly less than on modern pianos. By concentrating on the following procedures and by practicing them until they become habitual, one soon discovers that tuning early instruments is quite easy.

Relaxation and control are important, so one must sit in a comfortable position. The arm holding the the tuning hammer should be supported by the nameboard or the cheek of the harpsichord. The T-shaped tuning hammers are most natural on early instruments, but if a long gooseneck tuning wrench shaped like a piano-tuning hammer is used, it must be placed on the tuning pin so that its handle forms a parallel line with the strings as they angle from the tuning pins to the nut pins. This minimizes the ill effects caused by bent tuning pins. It is important to concentrate on rotating the pin in the bottom of its hole in the wrest plank (also called pin block) and to avoid bending or deflecting the pin from its natural position in the wrest plank. The bending of pins can prematurely wear out the wrest plank, and, worse, bent pins usually straighten out later to their original positions: This causes the newly-tuned strings to go out of tune. A good test to insure that tuning pins are not being bent is to remove the hand from the tuning hammer and strike the interval being tuned to see if there is any change in pitch. No change indicates good technique.

In learning to tune a harpsichord or other instrument, the tuning of two strings together should be repeatedly practiced. Two strings at the same pitch, one from each of the two eight-foot choirs, are preferable to use. Practice tuning these unisons in various locations throughout the range of the keyboard. An important rule of tuning is that before a string is actually tuned to the correct pitch, one should first unwind the tuning pin enough to make the flattening of the pitch perceptible. This serves two purposes: First, the ear is informed that the tuning hammer is on the correct pin. Second, any corrosive freezing at the bearing points is broken loose before raising the pitch. This prevents broken strings in two ways. While carefully flattening the string, notice how the unstable, wavering, or vibrato-like sounds known as beats become increasingly rapid and harsh sounding the more the string is flattened. When cautiously sharpening the string back to the normal pitch, listen to the beatings gradually slow down in speed. When the beating stops altogether or disappears, the harshness is gone and the strings are in tune with each other. It requires practice before enough control can be developed to stop turning the tuning pin at the precise instant the beatings cease. Usually beginning tuners continue right on past the point of no beating to the sharp side. Here one discovers that an out-of-tune string can beat just as harshly when it is sharp as when it is flat. In any case, a rule to remember is that when a string begins to beat faster than expected, this indicates that the tuning hammer is being turned in the wrong direction. Two more rules are: The interval must be played often enough so that the tone does not die away, and the tuning hammer must not be turned unless both strings are clearly being heard at the same time.

After enough control is developed to tune two strings together in a perfect unison without beats, one should practice tuning octaves, then fifths, fourths, major thirds, etc. While it is true that many musicians manage to temper fairly well by instinctively matching interval colors, a finer precision can be accomplished if the tuner can hear beats and control them, thereby being able to follow a temperament precisely. Only when this skill is mastered can one repeat the same temperament at will. The secret of applying this technique is always to be aware of the pitch location where beating is most clearly heard. This location, far-removed from the vicinity of the notes being played (except for unisons and octaves), is the place where the harmonic series of the two notes first coincide. One should study the table below so that one is not confused by softer beats that take place at other places of harmonic series coincidence. In the table below, when the intervals of the bass clef are being tuned, the ear should be concentrating at the locations notated in the treble clef. The beating at these locations is clearly heard when the intervals are tempered. When the intervals are tuned in just intonation, the beatings cease and the harmonics at the treble notations seem to disappear.

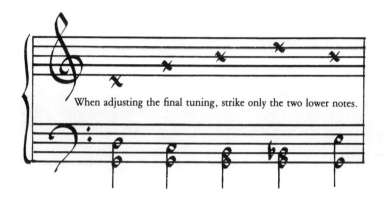

When adjusting the final tuning, strike only the two lower notes.

In using a tuning fork to establish the pitch of the first note in a temperament, strike the fork against your kneecap or the edge of the sole of your shoe, then press the handle end of the fork against the underside of the harpsichord where a scratch in the finish is not important. The whole harpsichord will act as a resonator for the tuning fork. Some tuners hold the handle of the vibrating fork in their teeth. The teeth and bony structures in the head carry the sound to the ear.

The customary order for tuning the various choirs of a harpsichord ensures that the most easily-heard or most stable areas are tuned first. This order is:

On double-manual instruments, the upper eight-foot.

On single-manual instruments, the front eight-foot (this is the choir plucked by the set of jacks nearest the keyboard.)

Choose a temperament and set it as directed on the strings in the middle of the keyboard.

Tune the remainder of this choir by octaves from the sample tones. Begin with the bass strings, then the treble.

Tune the other eight-foot choir in perfect unisons to the first eight-foot.

Disengage the second eight-foot choir just tuned, engage the four-foot choir, and tune these strings as perfect octaves to the first eight-foot.

An ultimate test is to engage all the choirs and play triple octaves chromatically throughout the keyboard. All octaves and unisons should be pure and beatless.

Following the tuning instructions in this book

With the exception of the classical piano concerto temperament, all the temperaments in this book are arranged to begin with middle C. If a standard pitch is desired, tune middle C to the C tuning fork. Otherwise you may tune middle C to any pitch lower that sounds good to you. Every note that is being tuned must be played with some note that has already been tuned. In this way, all adjustments are made while listening to vertical intervals and the harmonics that they produce. The temperament instructions are written in music notation. Quarter notes (crochets) symbolize the notes that have previously been tuned. Half notes (minims) symbolize the notes being tuned. The directions of the stems of the notes have no signifigance beyond helping the eye to identify the positions of the notes.

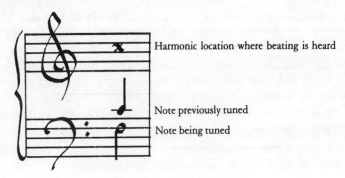

Harmonic location where beating is heard

Note previously tuned

Note being tuned

Every interval in the tuning instructions is meant to be tuned in just intonation with no beating unless specifically notated otherwise.

The Martin Agricola Just Pythagorean Tuning

The Martin Agricola tuning[1] is a transposed version of the much older Pythagorean tuning used during the Middle Ages. This transposed version was in common use during the fifteenth century, a hundred years before Agricola published it. It is called a "just" Pythagorean because the primary triads of A major are in just intonation. The virtue of the Agricola tuning is that the just intonation triads are among the commonly-used keys, while the wolf is placed in the uncommonly-used B-major triad. No tempering is done.

1. Martin Agricola. *Rvdimenta mvsices*. Vitebergae: G. Rhaw, 1539.

Henricus Grammateus
Pythagorean Temperament

This is called a "Pythagorean" temperament because ten fifths are still in just intonation and the natural keys are still in the ancient traditional Pythagorean tuning. The virtue of Grammateus's temperament[2] is that all the chromatic keys are meantones between their adjacent natural keys. In this way, ten of the semitones are all the same size, and the chromatic scale sounds like that of equal temperament. All twenty-four major and minor triads are good, so this satisfies the requirements of early composers such as John Bull who modulated through all the keys. Because of the bright-sounding major thirds and sixths among the natural or diatonic keys and because of the sharp leading-tones in C and F major, melody sounds superior in Grammateus. This temperament is an example of the so-called equal temperament that was practiced on sixteenth-century fretted instruments. Others who published this temperament were Juan Bermudo[3] and Friedrich Wilhelm Marpurg[4].

Tune F-sharp pure to D and then sharpen
F-sharp until D F-sharp beats at exactly the
same speed as F-sharp B.

2. Heinrich Schreiber. *Ayn new kunstlich buech*. Nürnberg: durch Johannem Stüchs für Lucas Alantsee büchfurer vnd bürger zu Wien, 1518.

3. Juan Bermudo. *Declaracion de instrumentos (musicales)*. Ossuna: Juan de Leõ, 1549.

4. Friedrich Wilhelm Marpurg. *Versuch über die musikalische Temperatur*. Breslau: J. F. Korn, 1776.

Salomon de Caus Just Intonation

In complete just intonation, only fifty per cent of the major amd minor triads are good. The remaining triads contain many wolf intervals. The Salomon arrangement[5] is the best because seven major triads from E to B-flat major can be connected by root movements modulating forward by fourths. The wolf in the G major triad is cleverly disguised either by leaving D unplayed or else substituting B or F for the D. In this way, the harmonic resources are expanded enough that much basic music in C major or A minor can be performed. Others who published this tuning were Marin Mersenne[6] and Leonhard Euler[7]. This tuning may have originated in the late fifteenth century. No tempering is done.

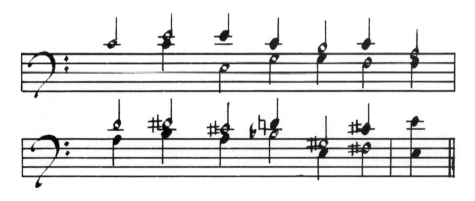

5. Salomon de Caus. *Les raisons des forces movvantes auec diuerses machines.* Francfort: En la boutique de I. Norton, 1615.

6. Marin Mersenne. *Harmonie vniverselle.* Paris: S. Cramoisy, 1636-37.

7. Leonhard Euler. *Tentamen novae theoriae mvsicae.* Petropoli: ex Typographia Academiae scientiarvm, 1739.

Pietro Aron Meantone Temperament and other meantone temperaments

In the meantone temperaments, only two-thirds of the major and minor triads are in tune enough to use for musical performance. In spite of this restriction, meantone temperament has had the longest usage in history of any temperament (including equal temperament). The term 'meantone temperament' is often taken to mean only Pietro Aron's temperament[8] because it was the most commonly used variety. Many varieties were published from the sixteenth to the late eighteenth centuries. Nine of these are outlined in *Tuning the Historical Temperaments by Ear*.

When all the major thirds in the instructions below are tuned in just intonation without any beats, Pietro Aron's meantone temperament will be the result. Experienced tuners who wish to apply their own personal good taste and who wish to use other varieties of meantone temperament may do so by adjusting the major third C E so that it is wide and beating any amount between one and seven times per second. If this wide major third beats more than seven times per second, well-temperament will be the result. In some of the historical meantone temperaments, the major thirds were tempered very slightly narrow. When this tempering by aesthetic judgment is done, it is essential that all the other major thirds be tempered to the same degree as C E. A further refinement is to make sure that the major thirds, when played in sequence going down the scale from C E, also beat progressively slower by very small degrees.

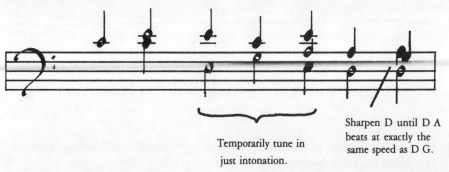

Temporarily tune in just intonation.

Sharpen D until D A beats at exactly the same speed as D G.

---

8.   Pietro Aaron. *Thoscannello de la mvsica*. Vinegia: Impressa per B. et M. de Uitali, 1523.

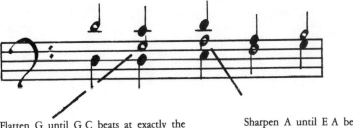

Flatten G until G C beats at exactly the same speed as D G.

Sharpen A until E A beats at exactly the same speed as A D.

Consult the tuning charts below and then continue to tune the instrument according to the key signature of the music that will be performed. Occasionally the music sounds better in a closely-related key. For example, some pieces written in C minor sound better when the instrument is tuned in either G minor or F minor. If the music does not sound good when the instrument is tuned in the tonic key or its closely-related keys, then the instrument should be tuned in one of the well-temperaments.

An enharmonic note is one that can serve as either a sharp or a flat, according to the key signature of the music being played. In the meantone temperament, none of the raised keys are enharmonic. For example, one can tune the raised key between F and G to be either F-sharp or G-flat. But if tuned as F-sharp it makes a wolf when played with B-flat. If tuned as G-flat it makes a wolf when played with D.

Because of this limitation of meantone temperament, it is tuned in two stages. The first is to tune all the natural keys. The second is to decide which raised keys are to be sharps and which are to be flats (based on the music to be performed) and to tune them as just intonation thirds according to one's decision.

The chart below shows the two possibilities for each of the five raised keys on the standard keyboard.

B-flat or A-sharp
E-flat or D-sharp
A-flat or G-sharp
D-flat or C-sharp
G-flat or F-sharp

In traditional meantone, one would select B-flat, E-flat, F-sharp, C-sharp, and *either* A-flat or G-sharp. It is also possible to tune B-flat, E-flat, A-flat, D-flat, F-sharp; or F-sharp, C-sharp, G-sharp, D-sharp, B-flat; or all five flats; or all five sharps.

Flats:

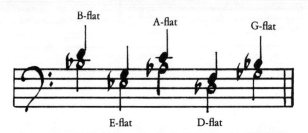

Sharps:

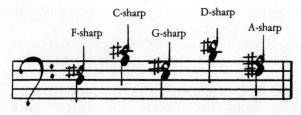

The Rameau-Rousseau-Hall Modified Meantone Temperament

This type of temperament was practiced in eighteenth-century France[9] [10] and England.[11] There are no wolf fourths or fifths. The sharps are favored over the flats. Even though the diminished fourths are improved enough to become major thirds, the intervals E-flat G, A-flat C, and D-flat F still sound too wolfish. Three-fourths or more of the harmony is considered good, so retuning for various key signatures is rarely necessary. By contrast, only two-thirds of the harmony is good in the standard meantone temperament.

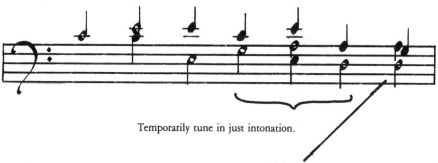

Temporarily tune in just intonation.

Sharpen D until D A beats at exactly the same speed as D G.

9.   Jean-Philippe Rameau. *Nouveau Systeme De Musique Theorique*. Paris: Ballard, 1726.

10. Jean Jacques Rousseau. *Dictionnaire De Musique*. Paris: Chez Lefevre Libraire, 1859. First printed in 1767.

11. William Henry Hall. *Encyclopedia, or Complete Modern Universal Dictionary of Arts and Sciences*. London: C. Cooke, 1797. First printed in 1788.

Flatten G until G C beats at exactly the same speed as D G.

Sharpen A until E A beats at exactly the same speed as A D.

Tune F-sharp pure to D and then sharpen F-sharp until D F-sharp beats at exactly the same speed as F-sharp B.

Tune F pure to B-flat and then sharpen F until B-flat F beats at exactly the same speed as C F. B-flat F is wide and C F is narrow.

Tune B-flat pure to G-flat and then sharpen B-flat until G-flat B-flat beats at exactly the same speed as B-flat D.

Tune G-sharp pure to E and then sharpen E until E G-sharp beats at exactly the same speed as the neighboring major third F A.

Tune D-sharp pure to G-sharp and then sharpen D-sharp until D-sharp G-sharp beats at exactly the same speed as D-sharp A-sharp. D-sharp G-sharp is narrow and D-sharp A-sharp is wide.

Tune C-sharp pure to G-sharp and then sharpen C-sharp until G-sharp C-sharp beats at exactly the same speed as F-sharp C-sharp.

Well-Temperament

Andreas Werckmeister (1645-1706) was an organist, composer, and theorist highly respected by Buxtehude, Handel, and many others. His writings influenced the temperament traditions of seventeenth- and eighteenth-century Germany more than any other theorist. According to Werckmeister, well-temperament[12] is a philosophy which holds that since the tonalities with the fewest sharps and flats are used the most, they should sound the best at the expense of the tonalities with many sharps and flats. Even so, the harshest-sounding triads from C-sharp major or F-sharp major should still be musical enough to use in performance. This means that modulations or transpositions are unrestricted. All twenty-four major and minor keys are musical. Also, there must be key-color changes during modulations, and the affects from the tonalities must differ.

When Werckmeister published his theories, keys with the fewest sharps or flats were the most commonly-used tonalities, primarily because of the long-established tradition of meantone temperament. Later in the eighteenth century, even though composers had long since developed proficiency in modulating through all the keys, composers such as Mozart and Haydn continued to use key signatures with very few sharps or flats in the majority of their compositions. This is because Werckmeister's philosophy of well-temperament had become established in temperament practices and therefore keyboard music simply sounded better in C major and the other simple keys.

Well-temperament is not the same as equal temperament. Equal temperament lacks all the qualities of key coloration. Equal temperament was known and tried many times from the sixteenth century on, but until roughly 1815 most musicians

---

12. In Werckmeister's *Musicalische Temperatur,* 1691, the term is "wol temperirt stimen." Although this translates literally as "well-tempered tuning" modern theoreticians, especially Barbour, distinguish between "tunings" — in which all tuned intervals are pure, and "temperaments" — in which at least one tuned interval is left impure or "tempered." To follow modern usage would give "well-tempered temperament," obviously awkward. I have consistently used the term "well-temperament" as a strictly technical term for the subset of unequal temperaments that satisfies Werckmeister's requirements for good temperaments. This is an unconventional use of the word "well," but serves as a constant reminder of the style of temperament intended by Bach in his *Well-Tempered Clavier.*

rejected equal temperament because of its harsh thirds in the natural keys and its lack of modulatory interest. Even as late as 1879, William Pole wrote:

> The modern practice of tuning all organs to equal temperament has been a fearful detriment to their quality of tone. Under the old tuning, an organ made harmonious and attractive music, which it was a pleasure to listen to. . . . Now, the harsh thirds, applied to the whole instrument indiscriminately, give it a cacophonous and repulsive effect.[13]

Today's custom of performing J. S. Bach's *Well-Tempered Clavier* in equal temperament is ridiculous because the purpose of the *Well-Tempered Clavier* was to demonstrate the key-color changes from one tonality to the next in well-temperament. If composers of the seventeenth and eighteenth centuries could hear their music in our equal temperament, they would judge our instruments to be out-of-tune.

The first five well-temperaments in this book are listed in the order in which the tempered fifths gradually beat slower. This places the Kirnberger temperament out of chronological order. The Kirnberger well-temperament divides the comma[14] into only two parts, so the two tempered fifths beat quite rapidly. The virtues of Kirnberger are that it is extremely easy to tune, and two of the major triads are in just intonation. There is extreme key-color contrast, and everything is in perfect balance.

The Bendeler well-temperament divides the comma into three parts, so the tempered fifths beat slower than those in the Kirnberger. There is much less key-color contrast than in the Kirnberger, but the keys with two or more sharps sound better. The balance of beatings on F A, G B, and C E is excellent.

The Werckmeister well-temperament divides the comma into four parts, so the tempered fifths beat slower than those in the Bendeler. There is slightly more key-color contrast than in the Bendeler, but the major third G B beats too rapidly compared to F A for good beating balance.

The Aron-Neidhardt well-temperament divides the comma into five parts, so the tempered fifths beat slower than those in the Werckmeister. There is much more key-color contrast than in either the Werckmeister or the Bendeler. The Aron-Neidhardt compares with the Kirnberger in this respect, but the graduations in key changes are much smoother than in the Kirnberger. The major third F A beats too rapidly compared to G B for good beating balance.

The Young well-temperament divides the comma into six parts, so the

---

13. William Pole. *The Philosophy of Music.* New York: Harcourt, Brace, & Company, Inc., 1924.

14. A comma is the mathematical difference between two inequalities that causes a wolf interval. The comma discussed here is the ditonic or Pythagorean comma.

tempered fifths beat slower than those in any of the above temperaments. There is more key-color contrast than in either the Bendeler or Werckmeister but less than in the Aron-Neidhardt or Kirnberger. The major third F A beats too rapidly compared to G B for good beating balance.

Johann Philipp Kirnberger Well-Temperament in C Major

Kirnberger[15] (1721-1783) was a theorist, conductor, composer, and student of J. S. Bach. Christian Ludwig Gustav[16] also published this temperament. Kirnberger's original was in G major.

Tune D pure to B-flat and then sharpen D
until B-flat D beats at exactly the same
speed as D F-sharp.

15. Johann Philipp Kirnberger. *Die Kunst des reinen Satzes in der Musik.* Berlin: H. A. Rottman, 1779.

16. Christian Ludwig Gustav, Freiherr von Wiese. *Der populairen Gemeinnützigkeit gewidmeter neu umgeformter formularischer Versuch über die logisch-mathematische Klangein theilungs-Stimmungs-und Temperatur-Lehre.* Dresden-Friedrichstadt: gedruckt bei der Wittwe Gerlach, 1793.

Johann Philipp Bendeler
Well-Temperament

Bendeler[17] (1654-1708) was a writer, clavecinist, and organist. In the original version of this temperament, the minor third B D was smaller than F-sharp A. This fault has been corrected in the following instructions.

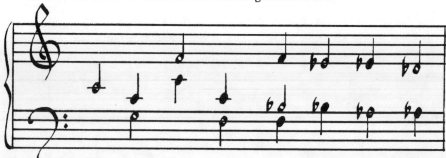

Tune D pure to F and then sharpen D until F D beats at exactly the same speed as D F-sharp.

Tune A pure to F and then sharpen A until F A beats at exactly the same speed as A D.

17. Johann Philipp Bendeler. *Organopoeia*. Franckfurt und Leipzig: In verlegung T. P. Calvisii, 1690.

Andreas Werckmeister Well-Temperament

This is most often referred to as the "Correct Temperament No. 1." In some books it is named "Werckmeister III."

Tune D pure to B-flat and then sharpen D until B-flat D beats at exactly the same speed as D F-sharp.

Tune A pure to F and then sharpen A until F A beats at exactly the same speed as A D.

Tune G pure to D and then sharpen G until G D beats at exactly the same speed as G C.

18. Andreas Werckmeister. *Musicalische Temperatur.* Franckfurt: In Verlegung T. P. Calvisii, 1691.

Aron-Neidhardt Well-Temperament

This temperament is named Aron-Neidhardt because many of the diatonic keys are identical to those of Pietro Aron's meantone temperament[19] and the remainder of the keys are tuned like those of Neidhardt's Sample Temperament No. 3.[20] This temperament is called Kirnberger III in several books.

Tune D pure to B-flat and then sharpen D until B-flat D beats at exactly the same speed as D F-sharp.

Tune G pure to D and then sharpen G until G D beats at exactly the same speed as G C.

Tune A pure to F and then sharpen A until F A beats at exactly the same speed as A D.

19. Pietro Aaron. *Thoscannello de la mvsica.* Vinegia: Impressa per ʹB. et M. de Uitali, 1523.

20. Johann George Niedhardt. *Gäntzlich erschöpfte, mathematische abtheilungen des diatonisch-chromatischen, temperirten canonis monochordi.* Königsberg: C. G. Eckart, 1732.

Thomas Young Well-Temperament

This is the "Temperament No. 2" by Young.[21] Temperaments similar to this were also used in eighteenth-century Italy.

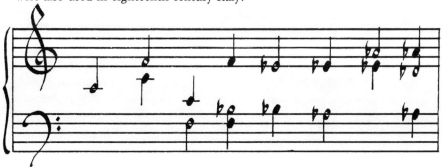

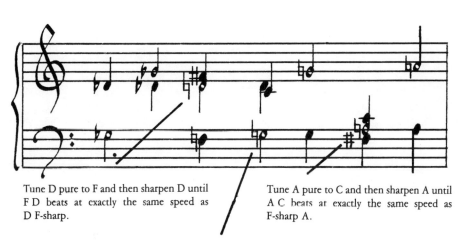

Tune D pure to F and then sharpen D until F D beats at exactly the same speed as D F-sharp.

Tune A pure to C and then sharpen A until A C beats at exactly the same speed as F-sharp A.

Tune G pure to D and then sharpen G until G D beats at exactly the same speed as G C.

21. Thomas Young. "Of the Temperament of Musical Intervals," *Philosophical Transactions of the Royal Society of London*, Vol. 90, January, 1800, p. 145.

Tune E pure to C and then sharpen E until
C E beats at exactly the same speed as E A.

Tune B pure to F-sharp and then sharpen B
until B F-sharp beats at exactly the same
speed as E B.

Common Model Well-Temperament (Bendeler-Young Composite)

Notice how similar this is to the Andreas Werckmeister. It is a synthesis of well-temperaments described by Bendeler[22] and Young.[23]

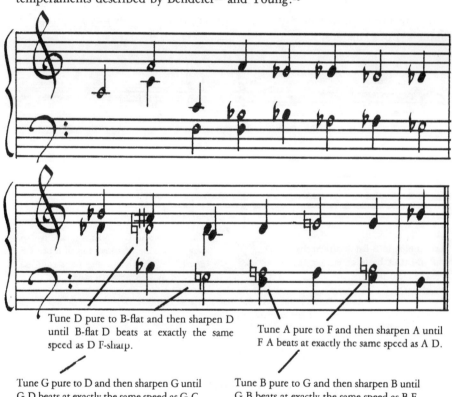

Tune D pure to B-flat and then sharpen D until B-flat D beats at exactly the same speed as D F-sharp.

Tune A pure to F and then sharpen A until F A beats at exactly the same speed as A D.

Tune G pure to D and then sharpen G until G D beats at exactly the same speed as G C.

Tune B pure to G and then sharpen B until G B beats at exactly the same speed as B E.

22. Johann Philipp Bendeler. *Organopoeia*. Franckfurt und Leipzig: In verlegung T. P. Calvisii, 1690.

23. Thomas Young. "Of the Temperament of Musical Intervals," *Philosophical Transactions of the Royal Society of London*, Vol. 90, January, 1800, p. 145.

Pythagorean Well-Temperament with Tuner Discretion

This is called a Pythagorean well-temperament because, as in the Aron-Neidhardt temperament which is strongly Pythagorean, the major third C E is allowed to be significantly more just than the other two primary thirds F A and G B. Also as in the Aron-Neidhardt, the transitions in key-color are kept very smooth and even. The basic philosophy is one of utility whereby the tonalities with a medium number of flats and sharps are considered as important as the simple key of C major.

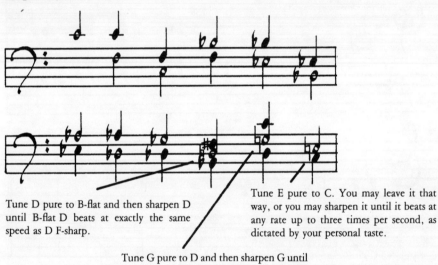

Tune D pure to B-flat and then sharpen D until B-flat D beats at exactly the same speed as D F-sharp.

Tune E pure to C. You may leave it that way, or you may sharpen it until it beats at any rate up to three times per second, as dictated by your personal taste.

Tune G pure to D and then sharpen G until D G beats at exactly the same speed as G C.

Tune A pure to E and then sharpen A until E A beats at exactly the same speed as D A.

Tune B pure to F-sharp and then sharpen B until B F-sharp beats at exactly the same speed as B E.

Just Intonation Well-Temperament
with Tuner Discretion

This is called just intonation well-temperament because, as in the half-comma Kirnberger temperament which is very just in C major, the primary thirds C E, F A, and G B are kept sounding alike. The basic philosophy is one of just intonation whereby C major is considered the one most important tonality, but modulations to all other keys are still possible.

Tune A pure to F. You may leave it that way, or you may sharpen it until it beats at any rate up to two times per second, as dictated by your personal taste.

Tune C-sharp pure to E and then sharpen C-sharp until C-sharp E beats at exactly the same speed as A-sharp C-sharp.

Tune D pure to B-flat and then sharpen D until B-flat D beats at exactly the same speed as D F-sharp.

Tune G pure to B. If the neighboring major third F A contains any beats, flatten G until G B beats at exactly the same speed as F A.

Classical Piano Concerto Temperament

This is like a moderated form of the Bendeler-Young Composite because the major thirds in D-flat major are less harsh and there is less key-color contrast. It is intended especially for use tuning a forte-piano (or a modern piano) which is to be used with an orchestra for piano concerti of the classical period. When the tuner uses an A-440 Hertz tuning fork to set the first note of the temperament, every note in the temperament except A is a very small amount sharp compared to the same notes in equal temperament. Since the orchestra tunes from the A on the piano, the piano no longer sounds flat when it comes in after the orchestral introduction.

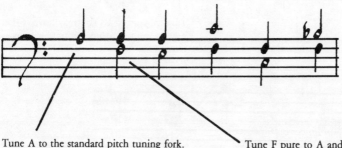

Tune A to the standard pitch tuning fork.

Tune F pure to A and then flatten F until F A beats three times per second.[23] This is 180 on the metronome.

---

23. By flattening F until F A beats at any rate between 3 and 6 times per second, an infinite number of well-temperaments can be created. These are like many of the temperaments published by Johann George Neidhardt, who died in 1739. The faster F A beats, the more like equal temperament the temperament becomes. When F A beats more than three times per second, the temperament no longer contains the virtue mentioned above which makes it particularly suitable for piano concerti. When F A beats less than three times per second, the temperament becomes distorted, with imbalances between F A and G B.

Tune C-sharp pure to E and then sharpen C-sharp until C-sharp E beats at exactly the same speed as A-sharp C-sharp.

Tune D pure to B-flat and then sharpen D until B-flat D beats at exactly the same speed as D F-sharp.

Tune D-sharp pure to A-sharp and then sharpen D-sharp until A-sharp D-sharp beats at exactly the same speed as D-sharp G-sharp.

Tune B pure to F-sharp and then sharpen B until F-sharp B beats at exactly the same speed as E B.

Tune G pure to D and then sharpen G until D G beats at exactly the same speed as G C.

Quasi-Equal Temperament
(Neidhardt-Marpurg Composite)

This temperament is the closest that it is possible to get towards equal temperament when only equal-beating methods are used. It is typical of the many early nineteenth-century temperaments that were called equal temperament. It is here named the Neidhardt-Marpurg Composite because the tempered fifths are the same ones that are tempered in the "Fifth-Circle Number Nine" published by Neidhardt[25] and the major thirds are fairly similar to those in the "Temperament A" published by Marpurg.[26]

Making sure that all the major thirds are wide, adjust both A and C-sharp until the major thirds F A, A C-sharp, and D-flat F each beat at exactly the same speed.

25.   Johann George Neidhardt. *Gäntzlich erschöpfte, mathematische abtheilungen des diatonisch-chromatischen, temperirten canonis monochordi.* Königsberg: C. G. Eckart, 1732.

26.   Friedrich Wilhelm Marpurg. *Versuch über die musikalische Temperature.* Breslau: J. F. Korn, 1776.

Tune G pure to D and then sharpen G until G D beats at exactly the same speed as G C.

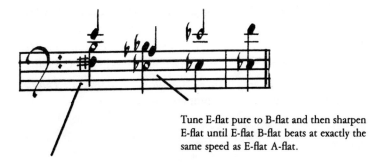

Tune E-flat pure to B-flat and then sharpen E-flat until E-flat B-flat beats at exactly the same speed as E-flat A-flat.

Tune B pure to F-sharp and then sharpen B until F-sharp B beats at exactly the same speed as B E.

Recommended Reading

Barbour, J. Murray. *Tuning and Temperament.* East Lansing: Michigan State College Press, second edition, 1953.

Boyle, Hugh, & Lloyd, Ll. S. *Intervals, Scales, and Temperaments.* New York: St. Martin's Press, second edition, 1979.

Di Veroli, Claudio. *Unequal Temperaments.* Buenos Aires: Artes Graficas Farro, 1978.

Jorgensen, Owen. *Tuning the Historical Temperaments by Ear.* Marquette: Northern Michigan University Press, 1977.

Kellner, Herbert Anton. *The Tuning of My Harpsichord.* Frankfurt am Main: Verlag Das Musikinstrument, second edition, 1980.

Klop, G. C. *Harpsichord Tuning.* Garderen, Holland: Werkplaats voor Clavecimbelbouw (distributed in the U.S.A. by The Sunbury), 1974.

Lindley, Mark. "Temperaments," *The New Grove Dictionary of Music and Musicians,* Vol. 18, pages 660-674. London: Macmillan Publishers Ltd., 1980.

Link, John W., Jr. *Theory and Tuning: Aron's Meantone & Marpurg's Temperament "I".* Boston: Tuners Supply Company, 1963.